Reflections of the Father

Robert A. C. Oliphant

Derrick L. Randall

For every mother who raises a man… every man who
becomes a father… every father who raises a son… every
son who becomes a father…

CONTENTS

International Christmas Ballard

Good Lord, Good Lord

America's Fears/ That Could Have Been Me

FATHER

… Pardon Me

One

Writer's Flow

Journey

Living

Quiet Alarm

Inner Breeze

Rites Of Passage

Visibly Unseen

Me

Family's Time

Jupiter

Self

Belief

Purpose

Not Too Bad

Choose

Unity

Refection's Hue

Robert's Introduction

I wrote these poems and created my collection to best represent my personality, and the qualities that I represent in others and myself. My poems are my own personal insights and feelings on subjects that I think should be talked about more. For example, my cinquain poem about Love represents my feelings of Love. Love can be surprising, but something you never forget. I can relate to this first hand. At times, I can find myself representing and loving something without acknowledging or realizing it's existence. Like myself, you may Love something or someone more than you know and take it for granted. In order to write these poems, I had to force myself to analyze how a certain subject made me feel and why. In some of my poems, I tried very hard to emphasize some of my valued traits, and how these traits can be displayed more in others.

- Robert

"You have only lost something when you have stopped looking for it."

– Robert Oliphant

Derrick's Introduction

I stumbled across some writings my son had put away. In reading his thoughts, I was engaged to write with him. Within deep contemplation, I decided to share our combined thoughts, as a book. I must point out Robert (my son) was in the ninth grade when he wrote these poems; however, he is sixteen years old, today. His words and understanding then surpasses my desire to reach within my talents at his age. It gives me great joy and humble acknowledgement to share this collection with you. I am optimistic the sharing of such a precious gift will stir your soul as it does my own in admiration. In the words of my son, Robert, "Dad, I know it will be great."

- Derrick

"It is one of life's greatest blessings to be a father!!"
- Derrick L. Randall

SON

Cinnamon Bun

Poetry is a warm delicate cinnamon bun.

Poetry is like the pleasant scent of spring flowers.

Poetry is about the gentle cool showers of May.

Poetry is as important as a gourmet pastry chef.

Poetry is as pointless as the morning sun.

Poetry means smooth and warm phrases.

Poetry is sweet.

-Robert

Identity (Robert the Giant)

I am like a giant lighthouse, guiding all lost ships to the

safe shore.

Beacon of hope to the hopeless, I am the Statue of Liberty,

or the Great Wall of China.

I am forever standing strong and protecting even when I am

weak.

What I lack in stature I make up for in spirit.

I'd rather be a scrawny giant, with weak arms but a strong

heart.

I am always important like the sometime's forgotten moon

carrying the tides like a strong man carrying his burdens.

I am like a strong and little, giant lighthouse.

-Robert

I am the One

Whenever I open my mouth, professors from universities

across the world rush to praise me for my genius.

I am so wise, owls come to me for advice.

I am the champion.

I sailed with Jason and the Argonauts, just so I could use

the Golden Fleece as a mere face towel.

I am religion.

I baptized John the Baptist.

I am ill when I caught the common cold I accidentally

spread the Bubonic plague by sneezing.

I am cool.

Whenever I back flip and sidestep, I create Hip Hop.

I am a trendsetter.

I started using my left hand for only three days and now

everyone wants to be different.

I am horror.

I skipped down Elm Street, clipped Freddy Kruger's nails,

won a game of hide and seek with Jason and Jack the

Ripper , and then I punched Jacko in the eye and now he

sees no evil.

I am serenity.

I am the one Buddha and Mahatma Gandhi comes to when

they have anger issues.

I am swag.

Nike begged me to sponsor their shoes, and when they

were too shy to ask me for a new slogan idea, to calm their

worries I told them to, "Just Do It!"

I am will power.

I bravely opposed Adolf Hitler and when he tried to limit

me to his concentration camp, I focused even harder and

broke it.

I am free.

I borrowed the wings of Icarus and easily soared out of

Alcatraz while mockingly waving goodbye to Al Capone

and "Machine Gun" Kelly.

I am me.

The one, the only

- Robert

Someone Who will

My Mother will not do my homework.

She will not take my tests or exams.

She will not earn me A's on my report card.

My Father will not always remind to be courteous to others

or to show respect.

Neither will he make my friends nor support them for me.

He will not apologize to others for my mistakes, nor will he

always be there to make me understand where I went

wrong.

But, I do know someone who will.

My sister will not apply for my colleges, and she will not

get me my teacher recommendations. She is not responsible

for getting me into college, nor will she apply for my

scholarships.

My friend may not care if I do not accomplish my goal of

earning a M.D. and becoming a surgeon. He will not pay

my taxes or buy me a home.

I know someone who will.

Those around me will help me and support me through my

toughest times.

No one but one person can make my decisions or handle all

of my responsibilities the way I want.

This person is me.

- Robert

Gay Marriage

We told African Americans how to work.

We told Native Americans where to live.

When it comes to who Americans choose to spend their

lives with, there should be no limit to the freedom we give.

The image of Americans we want to control and distort it.

I guess if not everyone does it, it just cannot be supported.

-Robert

Love

Love,

Unexpected, unforgettable, inescapable, nurturing,

supporting, protecting

Creeping up on you like a hungry lioness

Love.

- Robert

Untitled

I wish I could jump,

right into a brand new life.

Where no one is terribly sad,

some people here are ill.

Sick, hungry, and can't even read.

The life of a poor pig is not one I want to lead.

- Robert

The Rundown House

The house is pale and gray like a cloud before a storm.

On a windy day it sounds like the creaking of floorboards.

It tastes like bittersweet memories.

It smells like mold, mildew, and mothballs.

The house feels like a place that will stand forever.

- Robert

Smiles

The sun is like a beautiful spring.

The sun is the bright flame that signifies blooming flowers.

An orange is like warm summer.

An orange is colorful and sweet like the rainbows after a

summer shower.

The sun is like a lion.

It raises its golden royal mane when it wakes.

An orange is like mountain dew

The inside is bright and sweet.

- Robert

Where I' m From

I am from an iron
from Magic starch and snazzy steam-pressed slacks
I am from the rickety man made kiddie playground in a
messy backyard.
Old fashioned, overwhelmingly bright, it looked like it was
a playground for clowns.
I am from the soft Begonias
the Palm tree, whose slender frame flaunts its fan-like
leaves and casts a cool shade.
I' m from the large Sunday family feasts and generosity
from Robert Beckham and Ann Oliphant
I'm from the honest hard workers and the "you didn't hear
this from me" folk, from "yes/no what" and "who are you
talking to?" when my tone is out of line.
I'm from "He rose from the dead to repent my sins", and a
hopeful Christian with a Bible's worth of scriptures I've
yet to learn.
I'm from St. Pete and Dartmouth Ave N.
"Chitlens" and Kings Hawaiian rolls.
From the leg of my stepfather scarred in war in Iraqi.
The "farewell" of my dad's trusty "Blue Baby" Cadillac
traded for another.
I am from the musty bin as old as I, buried under
memorabilia within the garage, containing a precious baby
book with photos of a jovial young me "playing" on the
sidewalk
I am from those carefree moments of my exclusive
childhood.
A path to be followed, a chip off the old block.

-Robert

Profound Myself

I wish to look deeper within… through introspection; until
I lose myself and have no recollection of whom I used to
inhabit and title with my own name.

Goals I wish to reach that were unreachable to the timid
and tame.

The spirit that is in you is strong as well in me. The dreams
I have may be obscure and possibly impossible to see
unless you view through the vision of the master of my
religion, which you can never be.

Do not despair in those who are imprisoned, but instead
rejoice in those who are free.

For you are made to live exceptionally with an imperfect
spirit that perpetually guides you in a lost world that is
helplessly divided into finding the missing and losing the
discovery.

It is your obligation to reach for the former without
climbing the latter.

Even if my virtues were to abandon me and scatter, I will
not cry insubordination. For, I know no form of separation
can carry me astray.

I will not be fooled by the foolish, but I will stay put and be
seen by the world cursed with blindness.

I know where I stand.
I have Profound Myself.

-Robert

Technique

What I'm writing may seem irrelevant to you right now,
but I promise to make this as elegant as I know how.

Imagine these lyrics gracefully entrancing you like a
dancer's style.
Feel yourself floating upwards and right back down let my
gentle words ease you into relaxation for a while.

Smooth and fluid go ahead and ask me how I do it?

Give me a paper and pen, but do not make me liable if you
get too attached to the words I write because each line is
valuable.

From my eyes, I can easily spot out that one true prize
insight.

I feel like I could tip toe on a cloud, jump off and take
flight.

I only notice attention when I am at its center; filled with
suave, poise, and subtlety could I be any gentler?

Swift enough to tap dance on the skinniest kind of pole-a,
too refreshing and sweet like grape soda.

Words so cool you are shivering and shook.
Had you in the palm of my hands before I brought in the
hook, my dignity is the best thing that you never took
accompanied with rhymes on point like a Dr. Seuss book!

-Robert

In this Moment

In this moment, I am cognizant of the environment around me.

In this place, I take notice of the blank walls that surround me.

In this world, I am hidden and conflicted yet peace has found me.

No escape from thoughts that pursue me, help me find the way out.

Wait never mind, without a shadow of a doubt I now realize I am at my best, secure and still free in this moment, in my mind.

If thoughts struggled fiercely as they do in my head, am I without peace of mind?

Because if so I would rather be dead

-Robert

Cold

The chill air cannot faze you unless you allow it.

Heartbeats are slower in the cold, so slow that they cannot
be counted.

Go block out the cold air outside or better yet ignore it.

Find a way to toughen your hide.

Do what you can to keep your heart warm inside.

I have heard it is a cold world, but I still doubt that it is true
because the sun is a reminder of hope, innocence and
warmth instilled in each and every one of you.

-Robert

Sonnet of Wind

Should the breeze blow north, west, south or east?

Will it always lament and send everything in flight?

Must it always howl like a savage beast, sending away the
leaves in flight?

As swift as possible the wind carries me, floating, floating
and floating with nowhere to go.

Yet calming, serene, almost free
This feeling is one that I wish to know

It shakes the trees and graceful flag.

The waves are carried and pushed to shore.

Against the force, near the ground the plants sag.

Without this wild, nature would be such a bore.

I never wish for this wind to still.

Liberation that comes with it is a new emotion I feel.

-Robert

Movies

Don't you just love the movie theater? Ah, that homely smell of overpriced popcorn in the air…You know, if you ask me I might have truly been born there.

No really, in the movies with the stars I feel like I belong there. Sure you have those jerks with their feet on the top of your chair. It may get annoying with their dirty shoes practically in your hair, but I never cared as long as I was at the movies.

It is too bad though that I never got to enjoy as an 8 day old baby the premiere of Adam Sandler in the *Waterboy.* I missed that movie by 8 days. It does not matter because a few years later I caught it on DVD anyways.

It was the movie to see or at least I imagine I was told. Back when I was young Adam Sandler's movies were comedy gold.

But what did I know? The movie theater was the one place I could go when I first developed the urge to splurge on sour patch candy accompanied with a large drink and I would laugh at the problems of Hollywood actors, as they attempted to think of a way to save the day, get the girl and . their happy endings.

The movies back then in who knows when? Maybe times after 1950, had enough packed action that usually gave you enough satisfaction to forget your 37 cents that you came in with an ear to ear grin of large width.

I wish I got to experience back then (in the good ole days). Scrounging up a couple of dollars and a friend and begging mother to let me ride my 2 speeder to the movies after I finished my chores to see the stars fight each other with mixed martial arts full of gore and kung fue-y, or even better going to see the premiere of an iconic *Star Wars* movie.

None of these experiences of course were actually mine. My best movie experiences, as a child, were at home outta my favorite cassette case and that suited me just fine. As young as I was,… anything I watched put a smile on my face.

No matter what however the movies will be that special place where family, friends and I can come together laugh, cry and fear with the stars in our own space.

-Robert

Don't Forget

Don't forget to enjoy the good things in Summer, like

popsicles and daisies.

Don't forget at night to watch out for the lunatics and

crazies.

Don't forget the warm clothes in Winter, like your scarf

and coat.

Don't forget you cannot sail on in the sea of life without a

navigator and a very big boat.

-Robert

What's Missing/The Void

I cannot remember what I am looking for, will I know
when I find it?
My subconscious whispers forget about it, but I try not to
mind it.
Help me look.

I cannot find it waiting patiently in my heart, nor can I
listen for it hidden in my ears.
It eludes me in my dreams, my brain cannot quite spot it.
I need a revelation.

It was not looking back at me in the reflection of my tears,
so I tried looking for it in my smile of elation.
I checked up above and then on my knees.
I searched below, still I cannot quite figure out where it
could possibly go.

It is gone now will I see it again? I do not know.
I am not sure if it was taken from me… because if it was
never given… how could it ever be took…

Things are taken away when one is punished…
I think I learned my lesson.

Silence, can no one else find it? Can no one answer my
question?
I think I will find it later in my story when it is time to
finish the last chapter, time to close the book.

However, until that day comes it will stay missing so right
now
Help me look.

-Robert

You Are Never Poor on Christmas

Merry Christmas to the destitute, I truly wish the best for
you.
I know you do not have much, but you are still God's
blessed, too.
To those who are lacking, worry not, right now it may seem
like little.
But later on it will be a lot.

Embrace your struggles, whatever they may be, for you
may find them taken by the reassurance of a tree, or a
present, or a hug or whatever you receive.

Just know that you are loved.
For everyone can take comfort in trusting in who is real up
above.
Even if you think that you may have it rough, someone else
is scared that he/she does not have enough.
Turn your back on self-pity, pain and regret, and open your
arms and smile to Love you will never forget.

-Robert

International Christmas Ballad

Feliz Cumpleanos, to that special star that never seems to
lose its shine even during the darkest times.

Merry Christmas to the decorations and songs with holly
jolly catchy rhymes
Mele Kalikimaka, to the precious tree so dressed and
unique we adorn in our homes

Meri Kuri, to the frosty winds that chill our merry bones

Kirismas Wacan, to each of my fellow man even if you do
not understand the language that I say this in

I hope your holidays are wonderful and you do not think
me a fool, but Merry Christmas or as the Swedish would
say, "God Jul!"

-Robert

Good Lord, Good Lord

Good Lord, Good Lord will I make it there?

To that forever blessed place, where the rosy-cheeked cherubs coax you to slumber with lullabies as gentle as falling leaves.

Good Lord, Good Lord will I make it there?

Where my wings will grow in and coast me into the horizon like the birds in the air.

Where I will soar into my golden years forever shedding joyful tears

To that place, Oh Good Lord, where I may rest my weary bones in a sanctuary that I may forever call my own.

And myself and those around me will lounge forever on royal thrones.

Where I may never have to be alone and live peacefully in a place where bigotry and violence is not known.

A place where love and kindness is forever shown.

Where I know all these beautiful feelings will be shared everyday.

Good Lord, Good Lord will I make it there?

If so, please show me the way.

-Robert

America's Fears/That Could Have Been Me

I would like to start off humble in my message, you see,
and if this bothers you make like a bumble bee and buzz
off.
Last thing I wanna do is go against my Lord or against my
nature, but we need to end this impropriety in my
generation and bring forth a new form of mature
stabilization in my patriotic nation that I full heartedly
support.
But it is my obligation to dutifully report that we will be the
bringers of our own obliteration if we cannot find it in
ourselves to bring about our liberation.
It is the Lord's will that like sentries, we will not abandon
our station. We will open our eyes and take in the reality of
the situation that we are facing.
How are we going to fix our future if we cannot repair our
present? How are we gonna teach kids that their skin color
is a blessin'…
How can we feel safe if our dutiful police are abusing
power to start shooting and arrestin'…
Dead young man, only 3 years older, had to face that
challenge in humiliation and misery.
Now we have young black men as hard as boulders
carrying themselves with chips on their shoulders.
Everyone you see all thinking that
could have been me.
I hear that "You get what you pay for…" my point does not
get across in that phrase, so I will just have to say more.
A young brother gets followed and shot because he paid the
price of crossing the street. Murderer cries self-defense
for killing a black boy and gets off "Scott" free. And you
just want us to calm down?
Forget about it, and take a seat? No!
This ain't sweet it is bitter, he was a martyr and catalyst for
a movement all over Twitter.
Just for black men to see,

feeling that could have been me.
At the mercy of a trigger, happy childhood icons waiting
for the sting and continuance of police brutality further
corrupting a young citizen's mentality.
All we want is a little justice for the people while all some
want is a little just us forget the people.
America is a project, so let us put in the work and get U.S.
an A for completion.
If we can all share the right kind of teachin', we could
finally learn something and give our future something
bigger than ourselves to believe in.
Time for you to look into the eyes of the people,
man to black man without having the urge to disrespect,
neglect, and spit on me.
I am not your sofa, so do not expect to plop right down and
sit on me.
Now I am by no means trying to victimize myself.
I only speak for myself.
I was raised to not see color, but I still do not see why
people can be so spiteful to one another.
As a minority, we had the major heroes and we miss them.
Others were so afraid of our progress and our dreams that
they dissed them.
W.E.B DuBois, Martin Luther King, and Malcolm X it
seems like we are waiting for someone great to step up
next.
Well stop waiting because your great, if you cannot see just
know that I do.
You just need to believe it, and let your own heart guide
you.
Sometime it is like the nation is divided in two, distraught,
broken hearted, and blue.
Alienate us all you want but you cannot deny it is true.
Even in this unbalanced system within a system, we still
hold on to the same American ideals that you do.

In God we trust, as one we stand, how can you fit in if you
torment your fellow man with the sickly darkness you let
your inherited good soul become enveloped in.
We have schools full of kids murdered in their own
country.
Young kids get to thinking that
could have been me.
Scratch that maybe I can get you to see from a darker yet
interesting point of view.
How would you feel dying by your own where you
belonging your home?
If you think like this occasionally as I do…
You too will be thinking
That
Could Have Been Me.

-Robert

FATHER

... Pardon Me

The expression of uninterrupted thought

The reflection of expressed feeling

The right to write

The idea within

The stroke of the pen

Liberation

The writer writes

The journey begins

-Derrick

One

Lean in and listen close.

This is not a fairytale.

This is a journey.

I may burn your eyes along the way, but it will benefit you

better than burning the bridge ahead.

The prevention of a sore behind and a hard head

Here it is, without further a do. Be the best you. Nope, that

is not it, but for right now, I am done. Remember, it is a

journey…

Exactly…

An individual one

- Derrick

Writer's Flow

It is pouring like lava. It is boiling over within.

Flowing like it will never end.

Caught up in the fire,

Flaming and scorching those within reach.

Tranquil like the sunset,

Steaming like a sauna relaxing sore muscles.

These words are not some jive hustle.

-Derrick

Journey

Consensual laughter

Wholesome joy

Contagious fulfillment

The soul release

The body cleanse

The heart transcend

Sitting in Grandma's lap

Holding Mama's hand

Becoming a man

-Derrick

Living

Living in peace can be hard.

Living in chaos is expected.

Living understanding both is a journey.

Believing in a dream is commendable.

Living the dream is tranquil.

Living is a gift.

Believing is instilled.

The journey is an undertaking.

The dream is God's will.

-Derrick

Quiet Alarm

Silence is loud.

Oh what irony, unheard and soundly

Loud is silence.

Oh what transparency, unseen and heartfelt

When nothing is said, the mind loudly conceives thought.

Ironically, a quiet purchase intrinsically brought.

-Derrick

Inner Breeze

Give a high-five.

Do not pound the wind.

Calmly, take it in.

Do not vehemently forsake the win.

Catch the drift.

Do not refrain from the breeze.

Walk the walk, occasionally falling to your knees.

We all feel it, so we all can lead.

-Derrick

Rites Of Passage

A thin line

A steep hill climb

The rising of the moon

The setting of the sun

The initiation

The process

Trust

And

Happiness

-Derrick

Visibly Unseen

If I am soulfully present

How am I physically unseen

If I am empathetic in understanding

How am I outright misunderstood.

If and How

Forever and Now

Interchangeable conceptualization

Crazy, traditional standardization

-Derrick

Me

I am in the world. I have a name.

I have a mother and father too.

I reply to certain things. I will reply when needed too.

Am I what the eyes see? Am I what the heart feels?

Acknowledge me and then repeat…

-Derrick

Family Time

The time spent right now.

The memories of then

Laughing from the heart

Smiling within

Family, a collective whole

The forever of when

-Derrick

Jupiter

In my zone

… thought…

Relaxing my mind

In my space

… thought…

Taking it all in

Grateful for the beginning

Confident in the end

-Derrick

.

Self

the simplicity of right now

the complexity of later on

the certainty of when

the hesitation of then

the formulation of reality

the deconstruction of the illusion

… Evolution

-Derrick

Belief

… I am invisible because I do not desire to be visible.

I am driven because I desire invisibility.

I am genuine because I follow my heart.

I am great because I define greatness.

I am because I believe.

-Derrick

Purpose

Without it, I am lost.

A part from it, I am alone.

Drifting with desire determined to hold on.

With it, I am finding.

Aligned with it, I am at home.

My Purpose

It is solace.

It is my own.

-Derrick

Not Too Bad

Uh oh, I did it again.

Whew, I just let go.

It is okay.

Disliking includes liking

I will try again.

Humbly insightful…

-Derrick

Choose

Never to land

Sailing feels so grand

Pinch me and I will pinch you.

A reality too true

The joy in doing what you choose

-Derrick

Unity

Watched a man fall down

Reached out my hand

Standing tall

Mindful of the fall

Who is he

I, my friend

You, them, us

All

-Derrick

Reflection's Hue

Everything is real

Unreal does not exist

If it's perceived

It can be conceived

Tomorrow or today

Yesterday or then

Reality or when

Reflective and within

-Derrick

Let It Go

… let everything go

Relax

Float

Soar

... let it all out

Project

Release

Welcome

Peace

-Derrick

Color or Hue

You ever wonder why yellow is brighter than orange, but

orange still shines through...

Has thought ever presented, why are there so many shades

of blue...

Then in reflection, you realize there are only one shade of

white and one shade of black...

Reflectively, we have no clue.

The glare of me, the blur of you

Colors are dismissive to our true hue.

-Derrick

Together On Three

Everybody wants to be happy, yet everybody can be selfish

in his or her wants.

Step back, true happiness is shared.

Individual happiness can be collective possibilities or

divided misery.

What is the goal...

A championship or a mvp...

-Derrick

Ambitiously

On my journey, I have learned to hold yesterday close.

In each day,

I am aware of Love's existence.

I cling to the precious innocence of engaging unadulterated

joy.

My journey is unique in it is my own. The proprietorship of

self- worth, I walk within

understanding assured in my intrinsic belief. I am neither

fearful nor factious.

I am driven, internally ambitious.

-Derrick

Same Thing, Differently Explained

If you do not act in the manner, I understand,

Are you wrong…

If I do not act in the manner you understand,

Am I right…

Are you right because you do not cuss…

Am I wrong because I cuss but, I do not fuss…

Think about it…

Two quarters or five dimes…

It is still fifty cents.

One and the same

Perceptively different

-Derrick

Fulfillment

a journey, a process, and a dialogue

transformation

togetherness, solitude, and peace

unification

individual thought

collective solidification

-Derrick

A Little Worked Up

Desire bubbling deep within

Heart rapidly palpitating

Soul rocking starvation

Intrinsic conversation

A much-needed longer

Drive

Internal hunger

-Derrick

What A View

You are pretty.

Why the attitude...

It distracts your beauty.

It offsets your hue.

The picture is faded

no display of you.

Deflect the stubbornness

allow your pretty to project through.

-Derrick

Soulful

Alone yet surrounded

Lost in the visible

There yet overlooked

Unseen in the now

Recognized yet unrealized

Conceptual in reality

Where yet here

Invisible in transparency

Delicate yet explosive

Wholesome and cursive

Love...

The intrinsic purchase

-Derrick

Out Of Here In A Few

Start the engine

Release the brake

Look around

Check the view

Ease out

Speed through

Exceed limitation

Rise within you

-Derrick

It Is In You

Feel your groove

Relax exude

Do you feel that

... that

It makes you want to

Come right back

... that

Your groove

So smooth...

Consistent latitude

-Derrick

"Hippie"

I am up, so I am writing

I am sky high, so my mind is flying

Searching the beyond, sky diving

What goes up, comes down

Soaring the space, parasailing in place

My feet never left the ground.

-Derrick

Passionate

I am let it rip.

I am coming straight from the hip.

I write what I feel.

I am words in the mirror.

Exactly… real

From my soul

Through my whole

Every bit of me

Unapologetic

For the world to see

-Derrick

Blessed

I can write all night.

It is just where I am at.

What... I got it like that.

There is no use to hold it back.

What was that?

No, it is not a come back.

It is just where I am at.

I am let it go.

Let the words flow

intoxicating and habitual

It is my show.

-Derrick

A Heap Of Helping

Watch this

Ham hock and chitterlings

Okay listen

Black eye peas and lima beans

Inward comprehension

Kool-aid and biscuits

Outward repetition

Food proceeded by soul

Wholesomely feed

Culturally breed

-Derrick

Momentum

Far from perfect

Close to wrong

Beyond imperfect

Standing by right

Wrong there

Right here

Life's directional

Atmosphere

-Derrick

Observation

I get lost sometime.

I figure what is the use.

I cry inside.

I laugh on cue.

I am human.

I am just like you.

-Derrick

Reflective

I want to shine through darkness.

Lead when I can no longer stand

I desire to comfort every soul.

Follow when there is no define whole

I long to be

Stand when I cannot flee

I have aspirations.

Deep rooted in unity

-Derrick

Revealed

Still on that journey,

Believing and fulfilling a destined purpose.

It is not always easy.

I am walking into forever.

Every now and then checking the weather

I need to be prepared.

I am not by myself.

Nope, this journey is shared.

Individual in sight, but my co-pilot is on my right

Grabbing the wheel.

-Derrick

Daddy

I watched you from afar, yet I emulated you
internally.
As I watched you, you watched me, as well.

Your unforgettable smile and slight headshake
acknowledged how proud you were.
My outward emulation of becoming a man quite
like you was my acknowledgement of how proud I was
to be your "Boy".

I am comforted in knowing over the years when you
said, "Thanks for everything!" it went beyond those
moments.

You were speaking for both of us.
The Father whose example was worthy of
emulation, and the Son emulating his Father, two
different individuals and two different titles, yet the
same common denominator...Admiration!
- *Derrick*

My Daddy relayed this to me once, and I have never

forgotten it, *"People will buy a newspaper if they now you*

are doing badly." He said, *"Son, it is up to you to give*

them something worth reading."

I share the same words with my children today.

Lock your doors, but open your hearts.

It is hard, but it is fair.

1LUV JWJ

Dad & Son… Out!!

www.ingramcontent.com/pod-product-compliance
Lightning Source LLC
Chambersburg PA
CBHW031525040426

42445CB00009B/404